Are L.A.'s Children Ready for School?

Sandraluz Lara-Cinisomo
Anne R. Pebley
Mary E. Vaiana
Elizabeth Maggio

RAND LABOR AND POPULATION

The research described in this book was conducted by RAND Labor and Population, a unit of the RAND Corporation, for the First 5 LA–RAND Research Partnership.

ISBN: 0-8330-3623-8

Book design by Eileen Delson La Russo

Published 2004 by the RAND Corporation
1700 Main Street, P.O. Box 2138, Santa Monica, CA 90407-2138
1200 South Hayes Street, Arlington, VA 22202-5050
201 North Craig Street, Suite 202, Pittsburgh, PA 15213-1516
RAND URL: http://www.rand.org/
To order RAND documents or to obtain additional information, contact
Distribution Services: Telephone: (310) 451-7002;
Fax: (310) 451-6915; Email: order@rand.org

Preface

This book was produced as part of the First 5 LA–RAND Research Partnership. In November 1998, the voters of California established First 5 LA as a result of the passing of Proposition 10. Effective January 1, 1999, Proposition 10 added a 50-cent tax to cigarettes and other tobacco products. The revenue generated from this tax was earmarked for programs that promote early childhood development for children from birth to age 5.

The Los Angeles County Board of Supervisors established the Los Angeles County Children and Families First–Proposition 10 Commission (now known as First 5 LA) in December 1998. The commission's goal is to use the funds generated by the implementation of Proposition 10 to invest in the health and development of young children in Los Angeles County. The First 5 LA–RAND Research Partnership was established

- to analyze data from Los Angeles Family and Neighborhood Survey (L.A.FANS)— a survey of 65 neighborhoods conducted in 2000–2001, and to disseminate research findings related to policy questions surrounding school readiness, childcare choices, children's health, the contribution of neighborhood characteristics to young children's well-being, and children's health insurance coverage, access, and utilization
- to facilitate access to L.A.FANS results and other data by developing and implementing a strategy for outreach to organizations, agencies, and community groups concerned with early childhood development in Los Angeles
- to develop standardized measures of school readiness, childcare choices, and children's health that can be used in other studies and evaluations.

Under the research partnership, the RAND Corporation and First 5 LA research staff collaborate on identifying key policy questions about which policymakers and the public need more information. Although First 5 LA also provides funding to RAND to conduct the analyses, RAND research staff carry out the analyses and are responsible for all of the findings and conclusions drawn.

More information about First 5 LA can be found at www.first5.org. More information about L.A.FANS can be found in Appendix A and at www.lasurvey.rand.org/.

The RAND Corporation is a nonprofit research organization providing objective analysis and effective solutions that address the challenges facing the public and private sectors around the world. Additional information about RAND and RAND research can be found at www.rand.org.

This book, which draws on information from L.A.FANS, is intended for a general audience interested in learning more about school readiness in Los Angeles County. The book should also be of interest to community groups, health services agencies, and other groups that want to support children by improving their readiness for school.

A more technical presentation of the results described in this book can be found in: Sandraluz Lara-Cinisomo and Anne R. Pebley, *Los Angeles County Young Children's Literacy Experiences, Emotional Well-Being and Skills Acquisition: Results from the Los Angeles Family and Neighborhood Survey*, Santa Monica, Calif.: RAND Corporation, DRU-3041-LAFANS, 2003. Online at www.rand.org/labor/DRU/DRU3041.pdf/.

The RAND Corporation Quality Assurance Process

Peer review is an integral part of all RAND research projects. Prior to publication, this document, as with all documents in the RAND monograph series, was subject to a quality assurance process to ensure that the research meets several standards, including the following: The problem is well formulated; the research approach is well designed and well executed; the data and assumptions are sound; the findings are useful and advance knowledge; the implications and recommendations follow logically from the findings and are explained thoroughly; the documentation is accurate, understandable, cogent, and temperate in tone; the research demonstrates understanding of related previous studies; and the research is relevant, objective, independent, and balanced. Peer review is conducted by research professionals who were not members of the project team.

RAND routinely reviews and refines its quality assurance process and also conducts periodic external and internal reviews of the quality of its body of work. For additional details regarding the RAND quality assurance process, visit www.rand.org/standards/.

Table of Contents

Acknowledgments

The authors gratefully acknowledge funding for this report from the First 5 LA–RAND Research Partnership. We particularly appreciate the support, collaboration, patience, and advice of Tim Heindl and Armando Jimenez at First 5 LA. We are also grateful to the National Institute of Child Health and Human Development and the National Institutes of Health Office of Behavioral and Social Science Research for funding the Los Angeles Family and Neighborhood Survey.

CHAPTER 1

What Is School Readiness?

What does it mean to say that children are "ready" for school? It means that children have developed social, mental, and physical skills *before* starting school that prepare them for classroom learning. They enter school ready and eager to learn.

School readiness has other dimensions as well: Schools must be ready for children, and families and communities must provide needed support and services. In 1997, the National Education Goals Panel (NEGP)[1] developed a three-part recipe for school readiness. The key ingredients appear in the box below.

School readiness is important for children, for their families, and for society at large. Children who are ready to learn when they begin school

- learn more quickly
- are more engaged in school and learning
- are more likely to stay in school and graduate
- have a greater chance of success in the workplace later in life.[2]

In addition, children who succeed in their early school years have more self-confidence, higher self-esteem, and a lower chance of being involved in crime or violence.[3]

School readiness also has important benefits for society. It reduces the costs of education because children who are ready to learn need fewer special education services and are less likely to repeat a grade. In the long run, society also reaps the benefits of school readiness through higher worker productivity, increased government revenue through taxes, and decreased need for social services.[4]

Evaluations show that effective programs to help poor children be ready for school can be very good investments.[5] The costs of operating such programs can be much lower than the long-term social and economic gains they generate for society.

Assessing School Readiness in Los Angeles

In this book, we look at the school readiness of Los Angeles County's children. We also investigate whether some areas or some groups of children differ from the average in systematic ways. For example, how different are children in poor neighborhoods from those in

Key Ingredients for School Readiness

Children's readiness for school
- physical well-being and motor development
- social and emotional development
- approaches to learning
- language development
- cognition (such as reading and numbers) and general knowledge

Schools' readiness for children
- a smooth transition between home and school
- continuity between early care, education programs, and elementary grades
- a student-centered environment focused on helping children learn
- a commitment to the success of every child
- approaches that have been shown to raise achievement for each student
- a willingness to alter practices and programs if they do not benefit children
- establishment of student access to services and support in the community

Family and community support and services that contribute to children's readiness for school success
- access to high-quality and developmentally appropriate early care and education experiences
- access by parents to training and support that allows them to be their child's first teacher and promotes healthy, functioning families
- prenatal care, nutrition, physical activity, and health care that children need to arrive at school with healthy minds and bodies and to maintain mental alertness

SOURCE: National Education Goals Panel.

affluent ones? And we consider the effects of children's home environment. For example, what can families do to help kids get ready to learn? Ultimately, we want to know where and how community resources should be focused to help the kids who need it most.

To begin to answer these and other questions, we use information from interviews conducted with families across Los Angeles County. The interviews are part of the Los Angeles Family and Neighborhood Survey (L.A.FANS), funded by the National Institute of Child Health and Human Development. The goal of L.A.FANS is to understand how children develop in the context of their families and neighborhoods. Appendix A describes L.A.FANS in more detail.

In 2000 and 2001, L.A.FANS interviewed families and children in a random sample of 3,010 households in 65 L.A. neighborhoods. L.A.FANS also gave standardized tests to children and mothers in these families. The study team will reinterview these families in 2005 to learn more about how neighborhood characteristics shape kids' lives.

Figure 1.1 highlights the factors that we examine in this book and the ways in which research suggests they may be related. We focus on two dimensions of children's home environment that research shows affect school readiness:[6] children's literacy environment and parenting practices. The home literacy environment includes the availability of children's books at home, reading to children, visits to the library, and the amount of television that children watch. Parenting behavior includes the degree of warmth parents show their children and their disciplinary practices. These two dimensions are shown in Figure 1.1 in the white boxes. Improving these two dimensions is a major goal of school-readiness programs (shown in the blue boxes) such as parenting classes, early childhood intervention programs, Head Start and other early childhood enrichment programs, public library reading programs, and efforts to improve childcare quality.[7]

We examine how these two dimensions of home environment vary across characteristics associated with major social groups in Los Angeles. The social characteristics we consider (shown in the shaded box in Figure 1.1) include mother's education, neighborhood poverty, immigrant status (as measured by mother's place of birth), and ethnicity. For example, how different is the home literacy environment for children whose mothers have not completed high school and those who have? In addition, we look at children's age and gender because they also may affect children's school readiness. Our goal is to help organizations and policymakers assess how the social groups they serve are doing on these two dimensions and to identify where the need for additional support is likely to be the greatest.

The social characteristics examined in the first part of the analysis are likely to be highly interrelated. For example, immigrant mothers are more likely to be Latino—because the majority of immigrants in Los Angeles come from Mexico and Central

Figure 1.1
Pathways to School Readiness

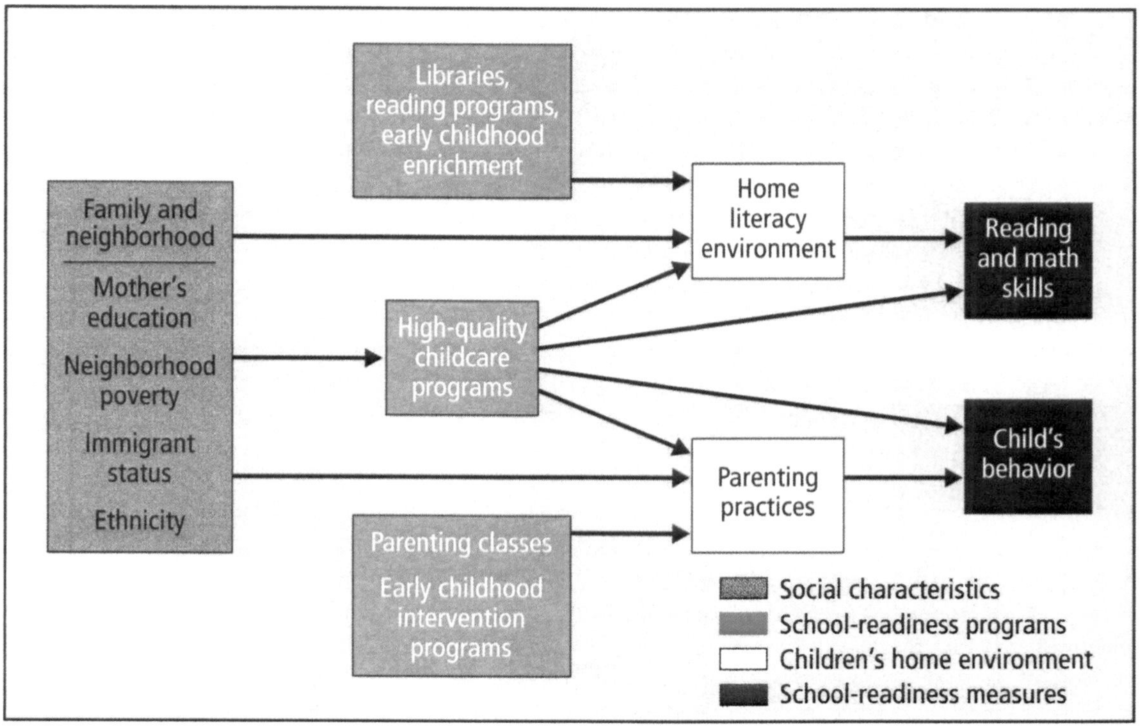

3

America—and less likely to be well educated. In the second part of the analysis, we attempt to disentangle these effects using statistical techniques that allow us to examine the effects of one social characteristic while "holding constant" the others. This part of the study has two goals.

First, we look at the effects of each social characteristic on school readiness "net" of other social characteristics. Our goal is to identify which social characteristics are the strongest predictors of school readiness. For example, is mother's education or immigrant status a more important predictor of a child's reading scores? Is ethnicity related to school readiness once differences in mother's education and neighborhood poverty are taken into account?

Second, we examine the association between children's home environment and school-readiness measures. Here our goal is to explore the potential scope for parenting classes, early childhood education, and other programs to improve the school readiness of disadvantaged children. For example, can parenting education programs mitigate the negative effects on school readiness of living in a poor neighborhood by promoting better parenting? Can improvements in the home literacy environment help to close the gap in school readiness between children whose mothers are less educated and those who graduated from college? We begin to answer these questions by comparing disadvantaged children from relatively poor home environments with children with the same social characteristics (for example, neighborhood poverty, mother's education, and immigrant status) who have relatively good home environments.

The primary goal of this book is to provide a basic description of school readiness in Los Angeles—a type of "report card" that the general public and organizations that focus on children can use to assess current levels of school readiness and to identify how groups they are most concerned with are doing. Understanding the root causes of school readiness requires a more in-depth study than the one presented here. However, by identifying social characteristics that are associated with school readiness and by examining the role of the home environment in these associations, we hope to inform policy aimed at improving school readiness and to provide information for community groups developing and implementing school-readiness programs in Los Angeles.

Our discussion is organized as follows. Chapters Two and Four examine the association of social characteristics with the

> **The primary goal of this book is to provide a basic description of school readiness in Los Angeles—a type of "report card" that the general public and organizations that focus on children can use to assess current levels of school readiness and to identify how groups they are most concerned with are doing.**

two elements of the home environment (shown in Figure 1.1 in white) that are our central focus: the home literacy environment and parenting practices. Chapters Three and Five assess the relationship of these aspects of the home environment and social characteristics with school-readiness measures (shown in Figure 1.1 in black). Specifically:

- In Chapter Two, we look at children's literacy environment—their access to books at home and in the library, how frequently adults read to them, and how much TV they watch.
- In Chapter Three, we examine how these aspects of children's environment relate to their reading and math scores. We also consider how various socioeconomic characteristics—such as neighborhood poverty, mother's education, and child's ethnicity—may influence these outcomes.
- In Chapter Four, we turn our attention to another important aspect of children's home environment—parenting practices that may affect children's behavior. In particular, we examine parental warmth and parental discipline.
- In Chapter Five, we examine how these parenting practices affect children's behavior, again considering whether better parenting can mitigate the detrimental effects of socioeconomic disadvantage.
- In Chapter Six, we discuss what our findings imply for communities and organizations that wish to focus resources on those children who most need help to be ready for school.

Because the developmental needs of toddlers (one–two years) are often different from those of preschoolers (three–five years), we discuss school readiness for these two groups separately.

In our discussion, we draw from an extensive literature in the field of childhood development. Key references for this literature, along with brief annotations, appear in Appendix B. Endnotes to each chapter provide additional references.

Throughout the book, we use tables and graphs to present the findings. All tables and graphs are based on data from L.A.FANS. We also use information from L.A.FANS to construct vignettes of children. These vignettes illustrate the wide range of children's experiences in Los Angeles and give readers more concrete examples of children's lives. They are composites of real children in L.A.FANS, but they do not represent any particular child, in order to protect L.A.FANS participants' privacy.

We present results for all of Los Angeles County combined. A select set of results for individual service planning areas (SPAs) within Los Angeles County is available in Appendix C. ■

CHAPTER 2

Home: A Place to Encourage Reading

Parents and family members are a child's first teachers. Young children whose parents read to them regularly develop stronger literacy-related skills before starting school.[8] They also learn to read earlier and progress faster once they get to school. Reading regularly to children gets children used to books and reading.

For parents to read regularly to their children, they must have access to children's books, knowledge about the importance of reading to children, time to read to children, and a basic ability to read. Public libraries make children's books available even to families who cannot afford to buy them. But some parents face more difficult challenges: They may have trouble reading themselves.

Do most young Angelenos have access to books? Are most kids read to regularly by family members? Which Angeleno children are missing out on reading activities at home? In this chapter, we look at children's access to books at home and in the library, how frequently adults read to them, and how much TV they watch. We also explore what other aspects of a child's environment, and what characteristics of the child herself, might play a role in these literacy activities.

What We Measured

We asked mothers to tell us about their children's literary environment. For example, we asked: "How many children's books does your child have?" "How often do you read to your child?" and "How much time does your child spend watching TV (or videos) on a typical weekday?" For the preschoolers (kids ages three to five), we also asked about library visits and how often parents talk with their child about TV programs. The L.A.FANS measures related to school readiness are described in Appendix D.

How many books should a child have? There is no right or wrong answer. Based on extensive research, the experts who developed these questions established three age-appropriate books as a minimum that toddlers need and ten as a minimum for preschoolers.[9] This is a relatively small number of books. Other studies show that children in middle- and upper-class families generally have many more books at home.[10]

How often should adults read to children to produce positive effects on reading ability? Again, there is no magic number of times. But research shows that reading to children *regularly*—whether done by a parent or by someone else—helps to develop reading skills necessary for later school success.[11] In our study, we looked at whether someone—parents, other relatives, or someone else—read to children at least three times a week.

For many children, watching TV can take time away from reading and other learning activities. Some television shows are designed to help children learn, but most are not. Experts recommend limiting television to a maximum of one hour a day during the week for both toddlers and preschoolers.[12] In our study, we looked at whether children watch more or less than one hour of TV per weekday.

Parents can make TV more educational by talking with their children about the programs they see. For preschool children, we looked at whether or not mothers talk with children about TV.

One concern about asking parents to report on the children's home environment is that they may report what they think *should* be true rather than what *is* true for their child. For example, parents may exaggerate how often they read to children or may minimize the amount of TV their children watch because they know that reading and limiting TV are good for kids. This problem is likely to affect our results to some extent and should be considered when interpreting our results. However, a number of studies have shown that parents' answers to questions in the Home Observation for Measurement of the Environment (HOME) inventory, a measure of the home literacy and emotional environment, do a good job of predicting children's subsequent reading skills, school achievement, and behavioral development.[13]

With this caveat in mind, in this chapter we look at how variations in social characteristics are linked with children's literacy environment. In the next chapter, we explore the relationships between the literacy environment and reading and math skills.

The Literacy Environment of L.A.'s Children

What kind of reading environment do young Angelenos have? Here's the overall picture (see Table 2.1):

- Most young Angelenos have several children's books at home. Eighty-six percent of toddlers have three or more children's books, and 75 percent of preschoolers have ten or more books.
- The majority of kids are read to by someone at least three times a week.
- Only about half of preschoolers visit the public library at least several times per year.
- Most L.A. children watch more than one hour of TV per day. Toddlers watch an average of 2.2 hours per day. For preschoolers, the average is 2.5.
- The majority of mothers talk with their preschoolers about the TV programs they watch.

Jamie is a two-year-old who lives with her mother in a small bungalow near the beach. Her parents are divorced and her father lives ten miles away. Jamie sometimes spends weekends with her father. While her mother Ruth is at work, Jamie spends the day at Brier Child Care Center near her home. At Brier, Jamie's day includes playing with other children, drawing pictures, lunch, reading books, and nap time. One of her favorite activities is being read to by a teacher or parent volunteer. In fact, Jamie enjoys stories so much that her mother usually reads to her before she goes to sleep.

	Has several[a] books	Is read to at least 3 times per week			Visits library at least several times per year	Watches TV less than 1 hour per day	Discusses TV with parents
		By mother	By others	By anyone			
Toddler (1–2 years old)	86	54	41	62	NA	21	NA
Preschooler (3–5 years old)	75	61	39	70	53	7	85

[a]Several means 3 or more books for toddlers and 10 or more books for preschoolers. NA is not applicable.

Many Angeleno children live in homes where reading and books are common. Nonetheless, there is clearly room for improvement. A sizeable number of young children are not read to regularly at home, have limited access to books, and watch more than the recommended amount of TV every day.

Socioeconomic Characteristics

We've drawn an overall picture of the literacy environment for L.A.'s kids. But are some families doing better than others? For example, are children whose parents are less educated or who live in poorer neighborhoods less exposed to books and reading?

To answer these questions, we explored how exposure to books and reading varied by mother's education, by neighborhood poverty level, and by mother's place of birth—in the United States or elsewhere.

Mother's Education

Mothers who have completed high school or gone to college have better reading skills. They may also understand more clearly how important reading is for their kids' progress in school.

Regardless of mothers' educational levels, most kids own some books. Even among children whose mother did not finish high school, 70 percent of toddlers had three or more books and half of preschoolers had ten or more (see Figures 2.1 and 2.2).

However, level of education seems to have a strong effect on parents' reading behavior. Only about one-quarter of mothers who did not finish high school[14] read to toddlers. Less than 40 percent of them read to preschoolers. In contrast, almost all mothers who went to college read to their children. Unfortunately, children of poorly educated mothers are less likely to have relatives and other adults read to them as well. For example, only 30 percent of children whose mothers are not high school graduates were read to by others, compared with almost 60 percent of those whose mothers went to college.

Figure 2.1
Toddlers' Home Literacy Environment Based on Mothers' Level of Education

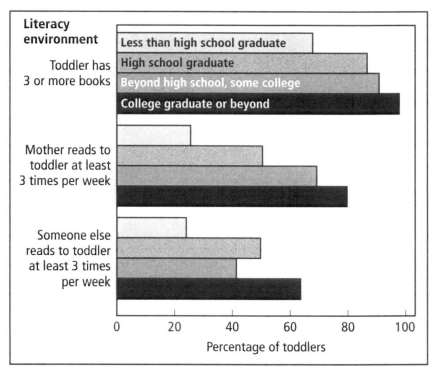

Literacy environment

Toddler has 3 or more books
- Less than high school graduate
- High school graduate
- Beyond high school, some college
- College graduate or beyond

Mother reads to toddler at least 3 times per week

Someone else reads to toddler at least 3 times per week

Percentage of toddlers

Figure 2.2
Preschoolers' Home Literacy Environment Based on Mothers' Level of Education

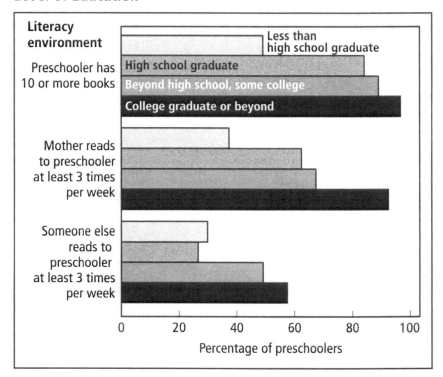

Literacy environment

Preschooler has 10 or more books
- Less than high school graduate
- High school graduate
- Beyond high school, some college
- College graduate or beyond

Mother reads to preschooler at least 3 times per week

Someone else reads to preschooler at least 3 times per week

Percentage of preschoolers

S am is a smart and energetic four-year-old. He lives with his parents and two older brothers in a modest apartment near downtown Los Angeles. Sam's father, Mike, works two jobs to support the family. His mother, Ann, runs a small convenience store on the ground floor of their apartment building. Sam spends most of his days in the store with Ann and even tries to help out when customers come in. If things get busy in the store or Sam gets tired, Ann tells him to go watch TV in the back room. Because of their busy schedules, Ann and Mike rarely have time to read to Sam. Ann also admits that she doesn't read books or magazines much herself and feels uncomfortable reading out loud. Sam's older brothers are not big readers either and are usually out at school or with their friends.

Neighborhood Poverty

Research suggests that children living in poor neighborhoods are less likely to acquire the skills they need to be ready for school.[15] Poor neighborhoods may have fewer libraries and bookstores than middle-class neighborhoods. Children may also be less likely to come in contact with adults and older children who read for pleasure.

To investigate the link between neighborhood poverty and reading activities at home, we divided neighborhoods in L.A.FANS into three groups: very poor, poor, and nonpoor—based on the average income of households in each neighborhood. Households in the very poor neighborhoods had an average annual income of $23,400 in 2000. Average household income was $33,900 and $55,400 in poor and nonpoor neighborhoods, respectively.

Figure 2.3
Very Poor, Poor, and Nonpoor Neighborhoods in L.A. County

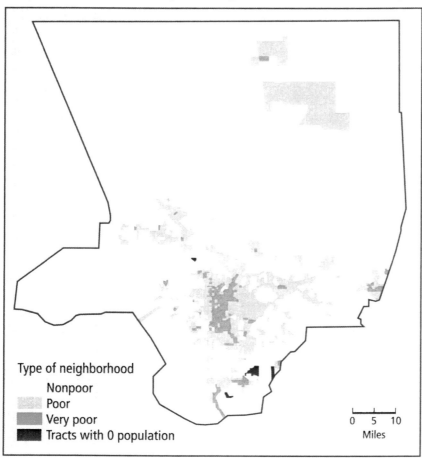

Type of neighborhood
- Nonpoor
- Poor
- Very poor
- Tracts with 0 population

0   5   10
Miles

Figure 2.3 shows how these types of neighborhoods are distributed across the county.

When we compared the reading behavior of children in these types of neighborhoods, we found that poverty is clearly linked with a less supportive literacy environment for kids (see Figures 2.4 and 2.5).

Both toddlers and preschoolers in very poor neighborhoods are less likely than children in other neighborhoods to have the recommended number of books. They are also least likely to be read to by parents or to visit a library.

The biggest difference in mothers' reading behavior is for toddlers. Toddlers in poorer neighborhoods are significantly less likely to be read to than those in affluent neighborhoods.

Mother's Place of Birth
Immigrants to the United States often face many challenges—including poverty, coping with unfamiliar customs and beliefs, and language barriers—that make functioning more difficult. These challenges may affect the kind of literacy environment that parents can provide for their children.

To explore whether immigrant status might affect a child's reading environment, we compared the children of U.S.-born mothers and those of immigrant mothers on the sorts of activities linked to reading behavior—e.g., children being read to, having books, visiting the library, and so forth (see Table 2.2).

Some striking differences emerge. U.S.-born mothers are much more likely to read to their children—the difference is especially marked for toddlers. Preschoolers whose moms were foreign born are much less likely to have books, or to visit the library.

These differences in mothers' reading behavior are "real" ones—what researchers call statistically significant. This means that the chance of the differences being a coincidence is very low (five percent or less). In contrast, the apparent difference in TV-watching between children of U.S.-born and foreign-born mothers is not statistically significant.

What accounts for these differences? Immigrant mothers may be less educated and may themselves struggle with literacy.

Figure 2.4
Link Between Neighborhood Poverty and Home Literacy Activities for Toddlers

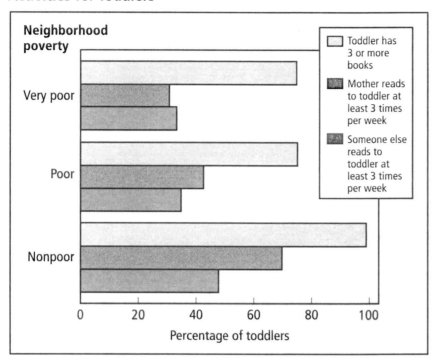

Figure 2.5
Link Between Neighborhood Poverty and Home Literacy Activities for Preschoolers

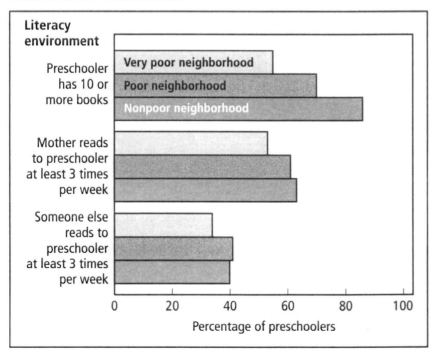

Table 2.2
Link Between Mother's Place of Birth and Home Literacy Activities

	Toddlers		Preschoolers	
	U.S.-born mother	Immigrant mother	U.S.-born mother	Immigrant mother
Mother reads to child 3+ times per week	78%	40%	66%	57%
Someone else reads to child 3+ times per week	53%	33%	47%	36%
Child has minimum number of books	96%	82%	94%	65%
Average hours of TV watched per day	2.2	1.9	2.8	2.4
Child visits library several times per year	NA	NA	60%	48%
Child discusses TV with parents	NA	NA	96%	80%

> **Immigrant mothers may be less educated and may themselves struggle with literacy. They may find reading to their children difficult or awkward. They may also know less about the importance of reading in developing children's skills and about the importance of books and libraries in their children's future school life.**

They may find reading to their children difficult or awkward. They may also know less about the importance of reading in developing children's skills and about the importance of books and libraries in their children's future school life.

Child Characteristics

We have been looking at several aspects of children's environment, including characteristics of their parents and the neighborhoods in which they live, to understand how they might influence kids' exposure to books and reading. What about characteristics of the children themselves—their gender and ethnicity?

We found no differences in reading behavior between boys and girls. But there are differences linked to a child's ethnicity (see Figures 2.6 and 2.7).

In all ethnic groups, most kids have access to an adequate number of books at home. But Latino and African American toddlers are less likely to have books at home than white and Asian/Pacific Islander toddlers.

Latino preschoolers are less likely to have access to books than other children. They are also less likely to visit the library regularly. Latina mothers are less likely than other mothers to read to their young children.

When we examined TV watching, we found that African American preschoolers watch at least one hour more, on average, of TV per day than preschoolers in other ethnic groups.

And virtually all parents report talking to their kids about TV programs.

Figure 2.6
Toddlers' Ethnicity and Literacy Environment

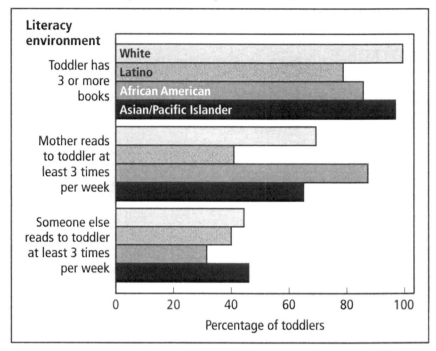

Literacy environment

Toddler has 3 or more books
- White
- Latino
- African American
- Asian/Pacific Islander

Mother reads to toddler at least 3 times per week

Someone else reads to toddler at least 3 times per week

Percentage of toddlers

Figure 2.7
Preschoolers' Ethnicity and Literacy Environment

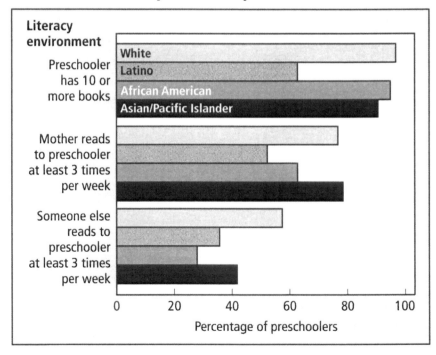

Literacy environment

Preschooler has 10 or more books
- White
- Latino
- African American
- Asian/Pacific Islander

Mother reads to preschooler at least 3 times per week

Someone else reads to preschooler at least 3 times per week

Percentage of preschoolers

The Literacy Environment of L.A.'s Children: In Summary

What can we conclude about the literacy environment for Los Angeles children?

Most young Angelenos have books, are read to regularly, and go to the library regularly. However, many others do not. Children living in poorer neighborhoods and those whose mothers did not complete high school are disadvantaged in terms of reading-related activities.

Latino children are particularly disadvantaged compared with other kids in early literacy activities. They have less access to books at home, are less likely to be read to, and are less likely to use the library regularly. Latino parents, especially recent immigrants, may be disadvantaged by poorer education, lower literacy levels, and language barriers.

In addition, we found that parents in affluent neighborhoods are not only more likely to read to their children, but they begin to read to them at younger ages.

Do these differences between families and between neighborhoods matter? How does a child's literacy environment relate to her reading and math skills? In the next chapter, we address these questions. ▓

CHAPTER 3

How a Child's Literacy Environment Relates to Reading and Math Skills

With encouragement from adults, kids find that playing with letters, numbers, and pictures is a lot of fun. Point to a picture in a book and ask "What's this?" and the child can't wait to tell you that it's a cow or a fire engine or a house. Reciting the alphabet as fast as she can becomes a source of pride. Ask a toddler to count the number of blocks in front of her, and she may have the answer before you finish the question. Like sponges, children soak up crucial skills from play and from everyday activities, particularly if parents help.

Children start building their reading and math competency early in life. If you read to a child regularly, she quickly sees that the pictures and words on the page are related to the story you are telling her. Later, she may surprise you by recognizing words even though she is not really "reading" them yet.

Children starting school with these basics are much more likely to succeed in school.[16] Have most Angeleno preschoolers mastered the fundamentals? In this chapter, we look at children's skills with words and numbers, and we explore some characteristics of their home environment that influence their skill acquisition.

> "The more children already know about the nature and purposes of reading **before** kindergarten, the more teachers have to build on in their reading instruction."
> — M. Susan Burns, Peg Griffin, and Catherine E. Snow, eds., *Starting Out Right: A Guide to Promoting Children's Reading Success*, Committee on the Prevention of Reading Difficulties in Young Children, Commission on Behavioral and Social Sciences and Education, National Research Council, Washington, D.C.: The National Academy Press, 1999, p. 15

> "Preschoolers who play games that involve simple arithmetic and geometry develop an intuitive math understanding."
> —Sheila Tobias, *Overcoming Math Anxiety*, New York, N.Y.: W. W. Norton & Company, 1995

What We Measured

We wanted to know if L.A. preschoolers had mastered basic reading and problem-solving skills that children their age should know. To do this, we asked the children to take two tests:

- A *reading test* that involved picture-word identification. For example, children were shown three pictures and asked to point to the picture of the house, or children were asked to match a picture to a word on a list.
- A simple *math test* that involved problem-solving abilities. Children were given instructions and then asked to find the information needed to solve a problem using simple counting, addition, and subtraction.

Our results are limited to preschoolers, because only those aged three to five took these tests. All tests were administered in English or Spanish, depending on the language in which the child felt more comfortable, and they were adjusted to each child's age. We also gave the children's mothers a standardized reading test. For more information about these tests, see Appendix D.

The reading and math tests that kids took were scored. Then the scores were "normed"—compared with a standard sample of children of exactly the same age who took the test when it was developed. Norming helps us to compare children of different ages using the same test because children are assigned a score based on how they did compared with children of their own age.

The normed scores have an average of 100. We divided these scores for L.A.FANS preschoolers into categories recommended by the researchers who developed these tests.[17] The categories are as follows: Scores of 111 and above are "high," scores of 90 to 110 are "middle," and scores of 89 and lower are "low." Children are considered to be performing at a level appropriate for their age if they are in the middle category.[18] In the national sample with which we are comparing Angeleno children, 25 percent are in the "high" category, 50 percent are in the "middle" category, and 25 percent are in the "low" category.

These scores are not absolute measures of school readiness. In other words, they cannot tell us whether or not an individual child has adequate skills to begin school. The scores do tell us how the child compares with a national sample of children her own age. They also help us assess whether children are doing worse than or better than children nationwide.

Toshiko is five years old and lives in an apartment building with her mother, Hiromi, in the South Bay. At the day care center, Toshiko's current favorite thing is working on puzzles. As soon as she gets to day care, out come the puzzles. She works with her friend to figure out where all the pieces fit. Toshiko also likes to sing with the other kids and play outside. The other day, their teacher, Mrs. Maloney, taught the children a song about colors and read them three new books. Hiromi is very proud of Toshiko because she can read beginners' books, can count to at least 100, and is pretty good at adding and subtracting.

Reading and Math Skills of L.A. Preschoolers: Overall Picture

First, let's look at how preschoolers are doing in Los Angeles as a whole (Table 3.1).

About the same proportion of Angeleno children (76 percent) are reading in the middle and high categories combined as in the national sample. However, fewer preschoolers in Los Angeles are scoring in the high category. For the math test, a larger proportion of children scored in the low category than for the national sample, although the difference is not large.

Table 3.1
Reading and Math Scores of L.A. Preschoolers (in percentage)

Category	Reading test	Math test	National norms (reading and math)
High	17	23	25
Middle	59	47	50
Low	24	30	25

Socioeconomic Characteristics

L.A. preschoolers' basic skills vary a lot, especially their math skills. Do family and neighborhood characteristics play a role in this variation? For example, do children in poorer neighborhoods have less mastery of reading and math than kids who live in wealthier neighborhoods? Do kids with better-educated mothers have better skills because these kids had more—and earlier—exposure to words and numbers than kids with less-educated moms?

To answer these questions, we look at the relationship between children's basic reading and math skills and both mother's education and neighborhood poverty level.

Mother's Education

Mothers with relatively little education may not be able to help their children master the fundamentals of reading and numbers. These moms may be struggling themselves with the basic skills or may not know how to teach their children these skills. Here we look at how well Angeleno preschoolers do on reading and math tests for mothers with different education levels (Figures 3.1 and 3.2).

Kids' test scores increased with moms' education. Roughly 70 percent of kids whose moms didn't graduate from high school scored in the middle and high range on the reading test. But nearly all kids did that well if their moms graduated from college.

A similar picture emerges for math scores. Roughly 60 percent of kids whose moms didn't graduate from high school scored in the middle and high range on the math test. But more than 90 percent did that well if their moms graduated from college.

Figure 3.1
Link Between Language Skills and Mother's Education

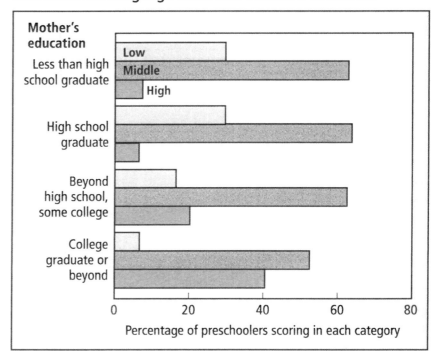

Percentage of preschoolers scoring in each category

Figure 3.2
Link Between Math Skills and Mother's Education

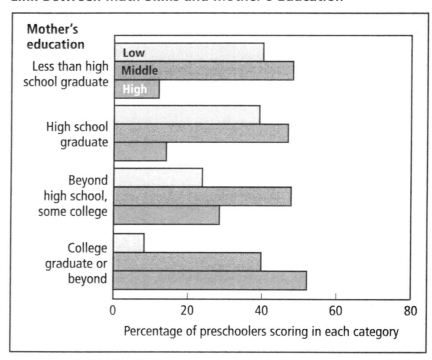

Percentage of preschoolers scoring in each category

The reading and math abilities of L.A. preschoolers are closely tied to their mothers' level of education. Even though lots of Angeleno kids performed adequately on both tests even if their mothers had little education, children of poorly educated mothers clearly have a harder time acquiring these skills. These findings suggest that children of poorly educated mothers are an important target group for school-readiness programs.

Neighborhood Poverty

Figures 3.3 and 3.4 show that children's skills are related to whether or not they live in a poor neighborhood.

Many more children in very poor neighborhoods have low reading skills than in the other two types of neighborhoods. Children living in poorer neighborhoods also have lower math skills than kids living in more-affluent ones. Roughly 60 percent of kids in impoverished neighborhoods scored in the middle and high category; 80 percent of kids in nonpoor neighborhoods did so.

Many preschool children living in neighborhoods where money is tight have poorer reading and math skills. Children in very poor neighborhoods are especially at risk for having low skills compared with children from other neighborhoods.

Mother's Place of Birth

Many L.A. County preschoolers have foreign-born parents. We looked to see if the mother's place of birth influences her children's reading and math skills. As Table 3.2 suggests, kids of U.S.-born parents are doing considerably better on both reading and math tests than kids of immigrant parents.

Figure 3.3
Link Between Language Skills and Neighborhood Poverty Level

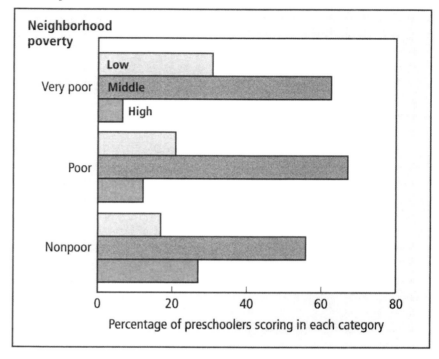

Figure 3.4
Link Between Math Skills and Neighborhood Poverty Level

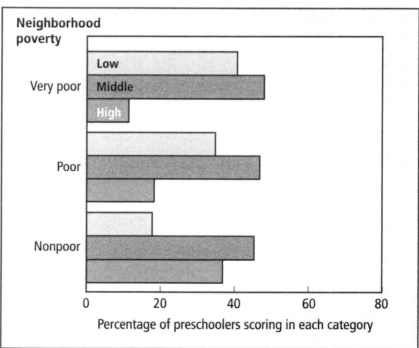

Table 3.2 Link Between Mother's Place of Birth and Reading and Math Scores (in percentage)		
Preschoolers scoring in the middle or high range	U.S.-born mother	Immigrant mother
Reading test	80	75
Math test	84	62

Juana and Nestor are three-year-old twins. They were born after their parents arrived in the United States and settled in the Pico-Union area. Their parents, Rosario and Miguel, have learned to speak some English and Spanish, but at home the family speaks K'iche', one of the Mayan languages. Neither Rosario nor Miguel went to school beyond the first grade and neither of them can read more than a few words. There are a few children's books in the house, which Rosario got on sale at the grocery store, but the twins are not very interested in them.

Child Characteristics

We also wanted to know how skills varied among different ethnic groups. We found that:

- Most preschoolers in L.A.'s ethnically diverse population have middle or high reading skills: from 73 percent of Latino children to 95 percent of Asian/Pacific Islander children.
- Most of L.A.'s ethnic groups have large percentages of preschoolers with middle or high math skills: 81 percent of Asian/Pacific Islander children, 75 percent of African American children, and 90 percent of white children.
- Latino children lag behind other kids in math skills—only 61 percent scored middle or high.

Most Latino children in Los Angeles have middle- or high-level reading skills, but they do more poorly on math skills. This suggests that an important focus for school-readiness programs may be helping Latino children to master numbers.

Reading and Math Skills of L.A.'s Children: What Really Matters?

Many factors seem to influence whether L.A. preschoolers enter the classroom prepared to learn. The poverty level of their neighborhood, their mother's education level and place of birth, and their ethnicity all seem to play a role.

If communities and organizations want to focus resources on the kids who are most in need of help, they need to know which factors are the most important. To identify these factors, we used a statistical technique that allows us to consider the influence of one factor while holding all the others "constant." For example, we can examine whether neighborhood poverty, by itself, is an important influence on kids' reading and math skills once we eliminate the effects of mothers' education levels. Or whether a child's ethnicity really makes a difference once we take into account neighborhood income and the mother's education. This kind of analysis can help identify potential policy levers available to decisionmakers who want to find the highest payoff use of resources.

We looked at two types of possible influences on reading and math scores: (1) socioeconomic characteristics (maternal education and immigrant status, the child's ethnicity, and neighborhood poverty level) and (2) home literacy activities (being read to, having books, visiting the library). We asked which of these, holding all other influences constant, are the most important predictors of doing well on reading and math tests and whether a child's literacy environment affects her scores.

L.A.FANS also asked mothers to take a reading comprehension test. As part of this analysis, we looked at the effect of mothers' test scores on children's performance. Mothers' own skills may have even more effect on how well their children learn basic skills than mothers' education does. For example, some mothers who are high school graduates read very well while others do not. Mothers who read well may be more likely to understand the importance of reading and may read more to their children. In this analysis, we can see whether mothers' education or mothers' reading skills are more important predictors of children's skills.

Figures 3.5 and 3.6 highlight findings from our statistical analysis. We conducted several different types of analyses to look at how different factors were related to each other. The results we present here are all based on an analysis that takes socioeconomic characteristics, mothers' reading scores, and home literacy activities into account simultaneously.[19]

In the descriptive results discussed earlier in this chapter, we saw that socioeconomic status (neighborhood poverty, mother's education, and mother's place of birth) are strongly linked to reading and math scores. However, if we set aside the effect of mother's education by holding it "constant" statistically, we find that neighborhood poverty levels are no longer a significant influence on reading and math scores.

Figure 3.5 illustrates the key effect of mothers' education. It shows how strongly mothers' education influences children's reading and math skills when other factors are held constant. Kids whose mothers had some college do significantly better than the national average on reading tests. Kids whose mothers finished college or obtained post-college schooling did significantly better in both reading and math. Well-

Figure 3.5
Children of Well-Educated Mothers Have Good Reading and Math Skills

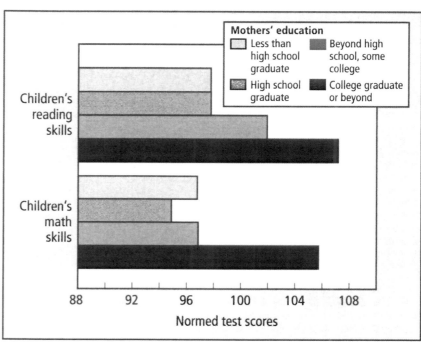

educated mothers, even in poor neighborhoods, are likely to have kids who do well on math and reading skills acquisition.

Mothers' education is important even when mothers' reading scores are held constant. In other words, the link between mothers' education and children's scores does not seem to be due entirely to the fact that more-educated mothers can read better themselves. More-educated mothers may be more likely to understand the importance of learning basic skills early—especially basic skills connected with school. They may also be more likely to understand the learning process and how to help their children develop the skills they need.

Once other socioeconomic factors are held constant, a child's ethnicity is not a significant influence on math scores. This means that if kids in all ethnic groups had mothers who were equally educated and had the same other characteristics, there would be no ethnic differences in math scores.

However, a child's ethnicity remains a statistically significant factor for reading scores, but only for Asians/Pacific Islanders. They do much better than anyone else even when all other factors are accounted for. We speculate that this may reflect the heavier emphasis that this group of parents—particularly immigrants—place on reading and education compared with other groups in our study.

We also found that children of immigrant mothers do significantly *better* on the reading test than native-born mothers' children, once mothers' own reading scores and socioeconomic characteristics (including education) are held constant. This may again reflect the strong efforts of immigrant parents to help their children get ahead.

These findings on ethnicity and immigrant status are very important. They suggest that school-readiness policy and programs should focus on the children of poorly educated mothers rather than on particular ethnic or immigrant groups. They also suggest that children of all ethnic groups and immigrant statuses can be well prepared for school if they are given the same advantages as children who already have good skills.

Figure 3.6 highlights our findings that home literacy activities are very significant—reading to children and visits to the library in particular. Here we are assessing how strongly these activities affect reading and math scores while holding constant other factors such as neighborhood poverty and mothers' education. Children who are read to at least three times a week or who are taken to the library at least several times a year have significantly higher reading and math scores. These simple actions that parents can take themselves can have a powerful influence on how well their children acquire critical skills.

Figure 3.6
Home Literacy Activities Are Important

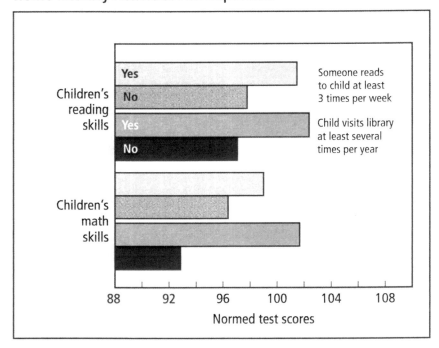

Our results suggest that early intervention and parenting programs that encourage parents to read to their children and to expose them to books are likely to have an important impact on school readiness—particularly for children of less-educated parents. Another approach, used by Head Start and other center-based programs, is to supplement home literacy activities with additional reading, exposure to books, and problem-solving tasks outside the home. Although we do not attempt to evaluate the effects of these programs, our results suggest that this approach may be particularly useful for children with poorly educated parents. ■

CHAPTER 4
Effective Parenting

Parenting strongly influences children's self-confidence and their ability to control their own lives—essential capabilities if children are to be ready for school. Parenting practices are also key to helping children learn how to behave appropriately in different situations. Parents who are consistently warm, loving, and supportive to children; who provide clear and reasonable household rules; and who enforce those rules in a consistent, reliable, and firm, but caring, manner are more successful at helping children to learn appropriate behavior. Moreover, discipline is likely to be more effective if it is appropriate to the situation and specific to the inappropriate behavior (e.g., telling a child in advance that she can't watch the video until she picks up her toys).[20]

Effective discipline does not demean or hurt the child and is "authoritative" and not "authoritarian." Authoritative means consistent, predictable, respectful, and calmly administered rule enforcement; authoritarian is more likely to be inconsistent, retributive, angry, and arbitrary.[21]

What We Measured

What kind of parenting behavior do L.A. kids experience? To answer this question, we used L.A.FANS data to examine questions from two standard measures of parenting: (1) measures of parental warmth toward their children and (2) measures of discipline.[22] (These questions are listed in Appendix D.) We focused on children one–five years of age.

The warmth measures reflect parents' answers to questions about: (1) how often they praised their child in the past week, (2) how often they hugged or showed affection to their child, and (3) how often they told someone else something positive about their child. The discipline measures reflect answers about: (1) how often parents spanked their child in the past week and (2) how often they punished their child by sending her to her room in the past week. Previous research shows that parents who report more warmth toward their children and report having to discipline them less often are more likely to have better-behaved kids.[23]

The relationship between discipline and behavior is not a simple one. Parents whose children exhibit more behavior problems already (perhaps because they simply have stronger personalities) may report less warmth and more discipline. Using data collected at one point in time, it's hard to tell whether warmth and discipline are related to children's behavior because difficult child behavior makes parents show less warmth and more discipline, or because parents who show less warmth and more discipline cause children to behave badly. However, studies that observed parents interacting with kids over time—and that also asked the same questions we asked—conclude that parents who report more discipline and less warmth are more likely to end up with kids who have behavior problems.[24]

> **Parents who are consistently warm, loving, and supportive to children; who provide clear and reasonable household rules; and who enforce those rules in a consistent, reliable, and firm, but caring, manner are more successful at helping children to learn appropriate behavior.**

It is also possible that answers to these questions reflect as much what parents think they are supposed to say as what they actually do. For example, middle-class parents may know that they are supposed to praise their children regularly and to use "time outs" instead of spanking. These parents may consciously or unconsciously overestimate their warmth and underestimate their disciplinary practices when responding to a survey. Developmental psychologists acknowledge the problem but say that there is nonetheless pretty strong evidence that these parental reports are related to children's behavior outcomes.[25]

With these caveats in mind, in this chapter we look at how variations in parenting behavior are linked with social characteristics. In the next chapter, we examine the association between parenting behavior and children's behavior.

Socioeconomic Characteristics

Parenting practices may differ by socioeconomic characteristics for many reasons. Less-educated mothers may have less information about child development. Parents in poorer neighborhoods may experience greater stress in their daily lives, which makes consistent and warm parenting more difficult. They may also have lower self-esteem and less confidence in their ability to accomplish things. There are also often cultural differences in expectations of children, attitudes to parenting, and parenting practices. For example, some foreign-born parents from more-conservative societies may see parents as authority figures and may feel that American-born parents spoil their children with too much praise and affection.

We found that parenting practices differ considerably by mothers' education. Less-educated mothers are significantly less likely to praise their children or to say something positive about their children to someone else compared with better-educated mothers. They are also less likely to hug or show affection to their child, although the difference is smaller than those for praising and saying something positive about the child (see Table 4.1).

In terms of discipline, mothers with less than a high school education are least likely to report spanking their child or sending the child to her room as punishment. For other mothers, however, the relationship between discipline and education is more mixed. Mothers who only graduated from high school are more likely to spank or send children to their room than moms who have more education or moms who have less than a high school education.

Table 4.1
Link Between Mother's Education and Parenting Practices (in percentage)

	Less than high school graduate	High school graduate	Beyond high school, some college	College graduate or beyond
Parental warmth				
Praises child almost every day	46	68	80	80
Hugs child almost every day	81	94	93	96
Says something positive about child to someone else almost every day	37	47	61	72
Parental discipline				
Spanked child at least once in past week	20	34	24	27
Sent child to room at least once in past week	32	56	42	43

In Table 4.2, we show the relationship between neighborhood income level and parenting practices. Two of the three measures of parental warmth are strongly related to neighborhood poverty. Specifically, parents in very poor neighborhoods are much less likely to praise their children and to say something positive to someone else about their child almost every day compared with parents in other neighborhoods. Parents in all three groups of neighborhoods are about equally likely to hug and show affection to their children.

Parental discipline is less strongly associated with neighborhood income. Parents in very poor and nonpoor neighborhoods are about equally likely to spank their kids, and parents in poor neighborhoods are less likely to do so. However, parents in nonpoor neighborhoods are more likely to send their children to their rooms as punishment at least once in the past week compared with parents in other neighborhoods.

Table 4.3 highlights substantial differences between foreign-born and U.S.-born mothers in parenting practices. Foreign-born mothers are considerably less likely to praise and say positive things about their children than U.S.-born mothers. They are also slightly, but statistically significantly, less likely to report hugging their child. As described above, foreign-born parents may have different attitudes about parent-child relationships (e.g., expecting their children to show them respect rather than affection). Foreign-born parents who are struggling to "make it" in a new society may also be under greater stress than U.S.-born parents and may have less time and energy for giving kids positive feedback. On the positive side, foreign-born parents are also considerably less likely to report spanking or sending their children to their rooms as punishment than are parents born in the United States.

Table 4.2
Link Between Neighborhood Poverty Level and Parenting Practices (in percentage)

	Very poor neighborhood	Poor neighborhood	Nonpoor neighborhood
Parental warmth			
Praises child almost every day	48	63	72
Hugs child almost every day	91	88	89
Says something positive about child to someone else almost every day	35	55	55
Parental discipline			
Spanked child at least once in past week	26	19	28
Sent child to room at least once in past week	34	39	45

Table 4.3
Link Between Mother's Place of Birth and Parenting Practices (in percentage)

	Foreign-born mother	U.S.-born mother
Parental warmth		
Praises child almost every day	57	78
Hugs child almost every day	86	94
Says something positive about child to someone else almost every day	46	61
Parental discipline		
Spanked child at least once in past week	19	34
Sent child to room at least once in past week	29	56

Table 4.4
Link Between Ethnicity and Parenting Practices (in percentage)

	White	Latino	African American	Asian/ Pacific Islander
Parental warmth				
Praises child almost every day	87	54	78	77
Hugs child almost every day	93	88	86	90
Says something positive about child to someone else almost every day	70	41	64	66
Parental discipline				
Spanked child at least once in past week	28	24	35	23
Sent child to room at least once in past week	50	40	55	27

There are also some ethnic differences in parenting practices (Table 4.4). Latino parents are least likely to praise their children or to say something positive about their children to others, perhaps reflecting cultural values about the importance of children's showing respect for parents and a reluctance to "brag" about children. Although there are some differences between white, African American, and Asian/Pacific Islander parents, none of them is statistically significant.

African American parents are the most likely to report disciplining their children, either through spanking or sending the child to her room. However, white parents are almost equally likely to send their child to her room as African American parents are.

Parenting Practices: In Summary

Our look at parenting practices reveals that mothers' education, neighborhood poverty, parents' place of birth, and parents' ethnicity are all associated with parenting behavior. In the next chapter, we look at how these parenting practices relate to children's behavior. ■

CHAPTER 5

Well-Being and Behavior

Children's behavior can affect their readiness for school. Children who are withdrawn most of the time often perform poorly in the classroom. They are also less likely to participate in extracurricular activities and may have fewer friends. Aggressive children have a harder time in school because they act out, bully other children, pay less attention, and can be disruptive in the classroom.[26]

During their first years of life, children learn many skills that are essential for success in school, including controlling their impulses, acting fairly, and interacting successfully with others.[27] Kids who live in a warm and supportive home environment with clear and consistent rules learn these skills more quickly and easily. They also develop a stronger sense of self-esteem and belief in their own ability to accomplish things. Combined, these skills and attitudes help make children ready and eager to learn in school.[28]

We looked at two types of behaviors that can cause problems for kids in school. The first is *withdrawn, sad, or anxious behavior*—which psychologists call "internalizing behavior." For example, does the child say that everyone hates her? Is she anxious or sad most of the time? Does she feel that she just can't do anything right?

The second is *aggressive behavior*—which psychologists label "externalizing behavior." For example, is the child cruel or mean to others? Is she hostile and unfriendly a lot of the time? Does she lie or cheat? Does she bully other children?

How well prepared are young Angelenos for school in terms of their behavior? Are there groups of children with especially high levels of sad or anxious behavior and misbehavior? In this chapter, we look at which L.A. kids have behavior problems that may affect how well they adapt to school.

What We Measured

We asked parents about their child's behavior. The specific questions come from a measure known as the Behavior Problems Index

"Preschoolers are inherently joyful beings . . . so if your preschooler begins to not enjoy activities or a favorite food and it lasts for many days, it's a matter of concern."
— Dr. Joan Luby, Washington University School of Medicine in St. Louis, quoted in the *Los Angeles Times*, March 31, 2003, part 6, p. 2

"My son, 3, can be very aggressive. At the playground, he'll push kids out of his way or even strike them if they frustrate him."
— Parent quoted in *Parents' Magazine*, "Just a Phase," by Denise Porretto, April 2001

"If I take him to a birthday party or the playground, he clings to me the whole time. I hate to admit it, but it drives me crazy."
— Parent of a four-year-old quoted in *Parents' Magazine*, "Tune into Your Child's True Nature" by Ron Taffel, April 2000

"The teachers tell me that my daughter is shy. But my husband and I think she is pretty assertive and it's hard to deal with."
— Mother who recently immigrated from China

(BPI). We focus only on four- and five-year-olds, because the BPI was designed for these ages. The BPI measures many aspects of kids' behavior and collapses them into two scales that reflect behavior problems. The BPI is described in Appendix D.

We asked parents, typically mothers, whether or not a list of statements were true about their child. For instance, we asked parents how true it is that their child "felt or complained that no one loved her" or that their child "bullied or has been cruel or mean to others." We combined parents' responses to create measures of sad or anxious behavior and of aggressive behavior.[29]

Families vary a lot in how they think their kids should behave. Parents' culture and experience affect their expectations. For instance, some parents may feel that their child should be quiet and respectful around adults. Other parents may feel that the same child is too shy. Immigrant parents may feel that their children should act like kids in their home country, and not like "American kids." These different perspectives are important to keep in mind while reading this chapter because we are looking at how parents themselves assess their children's behavior.

The scales were normed using data and procedures from a major national survey.[30] As for reading and math scores, norming compares the behavior of L.A.FANS children with that of a national sample of children. There is no precise level of sad/anxious behavior or of aggressive behavior that indicates a problem. Instead, the higher the score on either scale, the more likely a child is to have serious behavior problems. To make the results easier to understand, we focused on children with the most behavior problems—those in the top 20 percentile of the national norm. This means that the children we focus on have more behavior problems than 80 percent of children in a nationwide sample. More information on these measures is in Appendix D.[31]

Ty is a lively and active four-year-old who lives with his mother, father, and sister in a new development in the San Gabriel Valley. During the day, Ty stays with a neighborhood friend, Naomi, while Ty's parents go to work. Naomi takes care of several children in her home every day and uses the money she makes to pay the rent. Recently, Naomi told Ty's mother that she will have to find another day care provider for Ty. Naomi says Ty gets angry easily and bullies the other children. He has even hit Naomi a few times. Ty's parents have noticed that he gets bored easily and has trouble sitting still. But they were surprised and upset when they heard what Naomi told them. They are now trying to find another day care center or neighbor to take care of him during the day.

The Behavior of L.A.'s Preschoolers: Overall Picture

First, let's look at the behavior of L.A.'s preschoolers as a whole. We found that:

- Twenty-five percent of children four–five years old have high levels of sad or anxious behavior and 22 percent have serious levels of misbehavior.
- Children are more likely to be sad or anxious than to be aggressive. This is important for parents, preschool teachers, and others who work with preschool children to know. Aggressive behavior is easy to spot. Sad or anxious behavior problems are less obvious and may be missed. Yet they can also affect children's performance both before and after they enter school.

Although most kids are doing fine, some children in Los Angeles County have more problems. We looked at characteristics of their environment that might account for these differences. Specifically, we examined how children's behavior might be linked to socioeconomic characteristics such as mothers' education or neighborhood poverty level.

Socioeconomic Characteristics

Studies suggest that the amount of education a mother has influences her child's development in many important ways.[32] Part of the reason may be that mothers with different levels of education have different parenting styles. Mothers who have more education may know more about child development. More-educated families often make more money, which they can use to provide high-quality childcare. Higher incomes may also reduce parents' stress, which in turn affects parenting styles.

However, we found that the rate of children's behavior problems—both sad/anxious and aggressive behavior—was not related to how much education their mothers have completed. We also found that mother's place of birth was not related to either type of behavior problems—children of immigrant and native-born mothers had the same levels of behavior problems.

Poor neighborhoods can be stressful and difficult places to raise children. Parents working long hours and multiple jobs may not be able to spend as much time as they'd like with their kids or to supervise their activities and whereabouts. Crime and violence make some poor neighborhoods unsafe for children and their families. Children may react to a threatening environment by becoming sad or anxious. Others may act out or become aggressive.

We looked at the well-being and behavior of children living in very poor, poor, and nonpoor neighborhoods:

- Most parents report that their kids do not have serious behavior problems.
- But kids in very poor neighborhoods are much more likely to be sad or anxious than kids in other neighborhoods. They are also significantly more likely to have aggressive behavior problems, although the difference is not as large as for sad and anxious behavior.

Sad and anxious behavior is a more common problem for children in very poor and poor neighborhoods than aggressive behavior. In contrast, kids in nonpoor neighborhoods are about equally likely to be sad/anxious or aggressive.

Child Characteristics

Are girls or boys more likely to have behavior problems? Are there cultural differences in parents' reports of children's behavior? To answer these questions, we looked at behavior problems for children of different backgrounds.

We found that boys and girls are about equally likely to have aggressive behavior problems (22 percent each). But girls are more likely than boys to be sad or anxious (31 percent for girls and 20 percent for boys).

Ethnicity has little effect on kids' behavior. Children of all ethnic groups, as well as children of immigrants and U.S.-born mothers, have about the same levels of sad and anxious behavior. However, African American parents are more likely than parents of other ethnic groups to say that their children have serious misbehavior problems.

The Behavior of L.A.'s Preschoolers: What Really Matters?

Overall, L.A.'s preschoolers are doing pretty well in terms of behavior. Less than one-quarter have high levels of behavior problems. However, the levels and types of behavior vary across the county.

Communities and organizations that want to focus their resources on the kids most in need of help must understand which influences on kids' behavior are the most important.

As we did when we examined what characteristics of kids' environment really affect their reading and math skills, we used statistical techniques to weigh the importance of various influences on children's behavior. We examined two types of potential influences: (1) socioeconomic characteristics (mother's education and immigrant status, the child's ethnicity and gender, and neighborhood poverty level) and (2) parenting behavior (warmth and discipline). We asked which of these, holding all other influences constant, are the most important predictors of avoiding behavior problems and whether parenting behavior is associated with children's behavior problems.

For this part of the analysis, we created an "index" of warmth by combining parents' answers to our survey questions about praising and hugging a child and praising a child to someone else.[33] We created a similar "index" for discipline by combining answers to questions about spanking and sending a child to her room. We looked at the relationship between these two indexes, the social factors listed above, and children's scores on the sad/anxious scale and the aggression scale. Readers are cautioned that these scales cannot be directly compared. See Appendix D.

We conducted several different types of analyses to look at how different factors were related to each other. The results we present here are all based on an analysis that takes socioeconomic characteristics and the parent warmth and discipline indexes into account simultaneously.[34]

We found that neighborhood poverty level has a very strong effect on kids' behavior, even when parenting behavior and other factors such as ethnicity, mother's immigrant status, and mother's education are held constant. Children in very poor neighborhoods are more likely to be sad/anxious and aggressive than are kids in other neighborhoods. This suggests that poor neighborhoods are the key predictor of children's behavior problems and more important than the other social variables we examined (see Figures 5.1 and 5.2).[35]

> We found that neighborhood poverty level has a very strong effect on kids' behavior, even when parenting behavior and other factors such as ethnicity, mother's immigrant status, and mother's education are held constant.

Living in a poor neighborhood may be particularly stressful for young children.

It makes sense to think that neighborhoods would influence teens' behavior because

Figure 5.1
Children in Very Poor Neighborhoods Have More Sad/Anxious Behavior

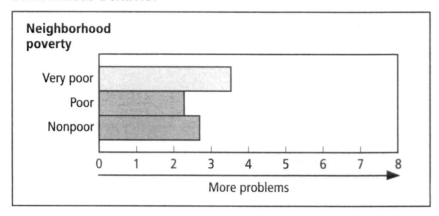

Figure 5.2
Children in Very Poor Neighborhoods Have More Aggressive Behavior

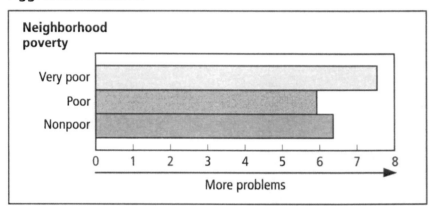

Figure 5.3
Parental Warmth Is Linked to Less Aggressive Behavior

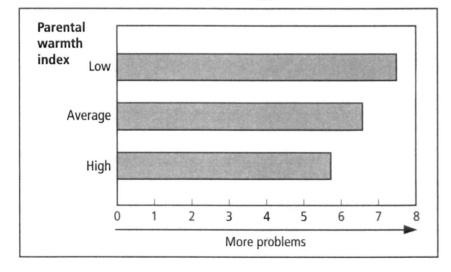

they spend much of their time outside the home. However, our results suggest that neighborhood conditions can also affect the behavior of young children. These effects may be indirect: For example, poor neighborhoods may increase stress levels of parents and older siblings. Or neighborhoods may affect young children directly by affecting factors such as whether they can play outside and the behavior of their playmates.

The only other factor that is significant is a child's gender: Girls are more likely to be sad and anxious than boys, even when all other factors are held constant. But boys and girls are equally likely to be aggressive.

When we looked at parenting behavior, as represented by the warmth and discipline indexes mentioned above, we found evidence that the way in which parents interact with their kids is related to kids' behavior. Holding constant social variables, children whose parents show less warmth toward them are more likely to be aggressive than kids whose parents have higher scores on the warmth index. On the warmth index, higher is better (see Figure 5.3).[36]

Parents' attitudes toward discipline also have an influence. Children whose parents scored high on the discipline index, where higher indicates more discipline, were significantly more likely to be both sad and aggressive (see Figures 5.4 and 5.5).[37]

It is important to remember that we can't really distinguish cause and effect between parenting practices and children's behavior when we use cross-sectional data (data all collected at the same time). Parents whose children are particularly aggressive and act out a lot may be more likely to discipline them and to show less affection to them *because* they act out. Or the fact that parents are more likely to discipline

Figure 5.4
Children Whose Parents Discipline Them More Have More Sad/Anxious Behavior

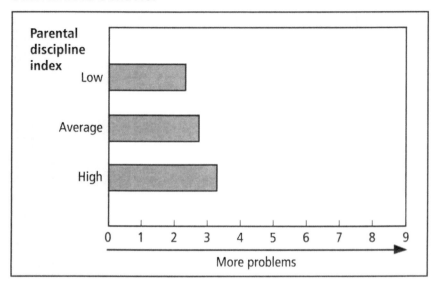

Figure 5.5
Children Whose Parents Discipline Them More Have More Agressive Behavior

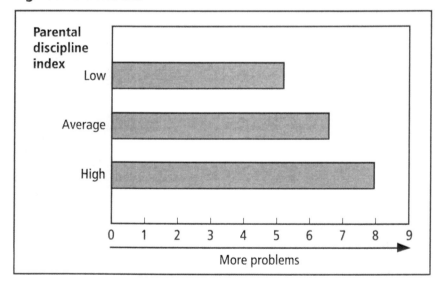

their children and less likely to show affection may cause the children to behave more poorly. Or both.

In the second phrase of L.A.FANS, we are looking at how parenting behavior affects children over the course of five years. This kind of information can help us do a better job of sorting out causality. For example, we can look at how parenting behavior earlier in childhood affects kids' behavior later on.

Whatever the direction of causality, it is clear that parenting behavior and children's behavior are closely linked. If children's behavior problems result in part from parental behavior, then parenting classes and family intervention programs may be useful. Other research suggests that it is possible to improve parenting through classes and interventions.[38] Parenting classes may help to prevent behavior problems by encouraging more-effective parenting practices from the start. But they can also help parents to develop better strategies for dealing with children who already have behavior problems. ■

CHAPTER 6

Helping L.A.'s Children Move Ahead

A s we outlined in Chapter One, school readiness is important for children, for their families, and for society at large. Children who are ready to learn when they begin school do better in school and are likely to succeed in adulthood. For society, school readiness may reduce the costs of education and help children stay engaged in school, graduate, and become productive adult members of society.

Our exploration of school readiness focused on how the home literacy environment, parenting behavior, and social characteristics affect two aspects of school readiness:
- basic skills, such as reading and math
- behavior problems, including sad/anxious behavior and aggressive behavior.

Our analysis shows that mothers' educational attainment and neighborhood poverty are the two social characteristics most strongly associated with school readiness. Mothers' education is a key predictor of school readiness. Children whose mothers did not complete high school are particularly vulnerable to having low reading and math scores. These mothers are less likely to read to their children, perhaps because they find reading more difficult. However, even if we hold mothers' reading scores and the frequency of reading to children constant, children whose mothers have more education do better. This finding suggests that mothers who are more educated may be more likely to value and encourage learning for their children.

Neighborhood poverty emerges in our study as a key predictor of behavior problems in young children. Children in poor neighborhoods are significantly more likely to have both sad/anxious behavior and aggressive behavior. Part of the reason may be that children in poor neighborhoods are more likely to come from poor families. Our analysis does not include family income. Therefore, we cannot assess what portion of the neighborhood poverty effect is due to living in a poor family. However, preliminary research using family income data suggests that neighborhood poverty remains an important factor in children's development in Los Angeles, even when family income levels are taken into account.[39]

On average, Latino and African American children and those who have immigrant parents score less well on reading and math tests than other children. The results in Chapter Three show that differences in socioeconomic status—particularly in mothers' education—account for all of the apparent differences among ethnic and immigrant status in basic skills scores. Ethnicity and immigrant status are not related to children's behavior patterns.

In other words, ethnicity and immigrant status themselves are *not* important predictors of school readiness, once differences in socioeconomic status are taken into account. In fact, children whose parents were born outside the United States do *better* on basic skills tests than kids with U.S.-born parents when socioeconomic status is taken into account. These results suggest that children of all ethnic groups and immigrant statuses can do very well on school readiness if they are given the same advantages as children who have good skills.

Our results also show that the home literacy environment and parenting behaviors significantly influence children's school readiness. Children who are regularly read to and visit the library have significantly higher reading and math scores. Greater parental warmth and less discipline are associated with fewer behavior problems for children. Thus, programs that succeed in improving parenting skills and the home literacy environment are likely to improve school readiness, even for children from disadvantaged families and neighborhoods.

These findings provide a pretty clear picture of the factors that affect school readiness. How can policymakers and communities use this information to improve school readiness? We did not attempt to evaluate how specific programs affect school readiness. Nonetheless, our study results may be useful to individuals and groups involved in formulating programs to improve school readiness.

School-readiness programs are generally based on two different strategies. One approach is to improve children's home environments directly. For example, parenting education programs[40] offered through nonprofit organizations, school systems, and other organizations teach parents more-effective ways to interact with their children. These programs also emphasize the importance of reading to children and other informal learning activities such as games, puzzles, counting, and drawing pictures. Home visiting programs bring professionals and/or volunteers into homes to work with parents and children on a regular basis.[41] Other efforts to improve the home environment include media campaigns that emphasize the importance of reading to children and programs that provide books to families. Libraries can also play an important role by helping families find age-appropriate books, organizing story hours and other reading-related activities, and sponsoring literacy programs for parents.

Another approach is to supplement children's home environments through early childhood programs outside the home. Children who are not exposed to reading and problem-solving at home can develop these skills in a high-quality preschool or childcare setting. Head Start and other preschool programs often provide parenting classes and encourage parent involvement. Thus, they may also improve the home environment. Some evaluations of programs such as Head Start suggest that they have relatively little effect. However, several well-designed studies of early childhood programs show that they can have an important effect on readiness for school and subsequent school achievement.[42]

Resources for school-readiness programs are limited. To begin to close the school-readiness gap between advantaged and disadvantaged children, it is particularly important to focus these resources on the children who need them most. Our study suggests that the children most in need are those whose mothers are poorly educated and those children living in poor neighborhoods.

Description of L.A.FANS

The Los Angeles Family and Neighborhood Survey is a study of the effects of neighborhood social conditions and family life on the growth and development of children. The project is a collaboration of a multidisciplinary team of researchers at RAND, UCLA, and several other universities nationwide. Funding was provided primarily by the National Institutes of Health.

L.A.FANS sampled 65 neighborhoods (census tracts) out of the 1,652 census tracts in Los Angeles County. The sample was based on a stratified sampling design in which poor neighborhoods and households with children were oversampled. However, with sampling weights, the L.A.FANS is representative of the population of Los Angeles County.

Within each of the 65 neighborhoods, households were sampled randomly (with an oversample of households with children). For each household, one adult was chosen at random by computer to provide basic demographic information for members of the household. When children were living in the home, one child and a sibling (from birth to age 17) were randomly selected to participate.

This book is based only on households with children from birth to age five. Of the 3,010 households included in L.A.FANS, a total of 1,720 included at least one child in that age range. Data were collected for 1,086 children. Of those, 717 (66 percent) were the children originally sampled from their household, and 369 (34 percent) were their siblings. All results in this book have been adjusted for oversampling.

Basic characteristics of L.A.FANS neighborhoods are shown in Table A.1 for very poor, poor, and nonpoor neighborhoods. Results for all L.A.FANS census tracts appear in the second to the last column. The final column shows results for all Los Angeles County census tracts combined. Comparing the last two columns shows that the L.A.FANS data, when adjusted for oversampling, are representative of the county as a whole.

Table A.1
Characteristics of L.A.FANS Neighborhoods

Characteristic	Very poor neighborhoods	Poor neighborhoods	Nonpoor neighborhoods	Total for all L.A.FANS census tracts[a]	Total for all L.A. County census tracts
% of population who are foreign born	50	50	25	34	35
% of population who are recent immigrants (since 1990)	20	18	5	11	12
Residential stability (% of population in same house five years ago)	48	50	53	52	53
% of households with income < $15,000	35	20	10	16	17
% of households with income ≥$75,000	8	12	35	27	25
Median household income	$23,000	$34,000	$55,000	$47,000	$42,189
% of families who are poor (below the federal poverty line)[b]	40	25	10	16	17
% of female-headed households	15	10	5	8	8
% of population that is white	5	15	49	36	31
% African American	16	6	7	7	9
% Latino	70	64	25	38	45
% Asian/Pacific Islander	5	9	16	13	12
% of other ethnic groups	5	7	5	6	3
Number of neighborhoods (tracts)	20	20	25	65	1,652
% of all L.A. county neighborhoods in this category	10	35	55	--	--

SOURCE: All data come from the 2000 U.S. Census.

[a]These averages were weighted to correct for oversampling and thus represent L.A. County as a whole.

[b]For a definition of the federal poverty level see www.census.gov/hhes/poverty/threshld/thresh00.html.

Brief Annotated List of Core References

Arnold, D. H., and G. L. Doctoroff, "The Early Education of Socioeconomically Disadvantaged Children," *Annual Review of Psychology*, Vol. 54, 2003, pp. 517–545.

Examines evidence from research on the effects of early childhood education on child outcomes for disadvantaged children.

Bowman, B. T., M. S. Donovan, and M. S. Burns, eds., *Eager to Learn: Educating Our Preschoolers*, Commission on Behavioral and Social Sciences and Education, National Research Council, Washington, D.C.: The National Academy Press, 2001. Online at www.nap.edu/books/0309068363/html/ (as of February 2004).

Describes new research findings on how young children learn and the impact of early learning. Explores the effect of these findings on policy.

Bradley, R. H., and R. F. Corwyn, "Socioeconomic Status and Child Development," *Annual Review of Psychology*, Vol. 53, 2002, pp. 371–399.

Provides an extensive overview of research on the effects of family and neighborhood socioeconomic status on children's development.

Bradley, R. H., R. F. Corwyn, M. Burchinal, H. Pipes McAdoo, and C. Garcia Coll, "The Home Environments of Children in the United States Part II: Relations with Behavioral Development Through Age Thirteen," *Child Development*, Vol. 72, 2001, pp. 1868–1886.

Describes the results of a long-term study of the effects of parenting practices and other aspects of the home environment on children's behavioral development.

Brooks-Gunn, J., and G. Duncan, "The Effects of Poverty on Children," *The Future of Children*, Vol. 7, 1997, pp. 55–71.

Provides a thorough overview, in lay language, of the relationship between poverty and children's well-being.

Burns, M. S., P. Griffin, and C. E. Snow, eds., *Starting Out Right: A Guide to Promoting Children's Reading Success*, Committee on the Prevention of Reading Difficulties in Young Children, Commission on Behavioral and Social Sciences and Education, National Research Council, Washington, D.C.: The National Academy Press, 1999. Online at http://books.nap.edu/books/0309064104/html/index.html (as of February 2004).

Examines ways to improve children's success in reading based on the latest research.

Chase-Lansdale, P. L., R. A. Gordon, J. Brooks-Gunn, and P. K. Klebanov, "Neighborhood and Family Influences on the Intellectual and Behavioral Competence of Preschool and Early School-Age Children," in J. Brooks-Gunn, G. J. Duncan, and J. L. Aber, eds., *Neighborhood Poverty: Vol. 1, Context and Consequences for Children*, New York, N.Y.: Russell Sage Foundation, 1997, pp. 79–118.

Examines the potential effects of neighborhoods on children's intellectual and behavioral development.

Karoly, Lynn A., et al., *Investing in Our Children: What We Know and Don't Know About the Costs and Benefits of Early Childhood Interventions*, Santa Monica, Calif.: RAND Corporation, 1998. Online at www.rand.org/publications/MR/MR898/ (as of February 2004).

An evaluation of the state of knowledge about the costs and benefits of early childhood intervention programs.

Linver, M. R., J. Brooks-Gunn, and D. E. Kohen, "Family Processes as Pathways from Income to Young Child Development," *Developmental Psychology*, Vol. 38, No. 5, 2002, pp. 719–735.

Describes the effects of poverty on family processes that can affect child development.

Maccoby, E., and J. Martin, "Socialization in the Context of the Family: Parent-Child Interactions," in E. M. Hetherington, ed., *Handbook of Child Psychology: Vol. 4, Socialization, Personality, and Social Development*, New York, N.Y.: Wiley, 1983, pp. 1–101.

Thorough review of the role of the family environment, including parenting, on children's development.

Shonkoff, Jack P., and Deborah A. Phillips, eds., *From Neurons to Neighborhoods: The Science of Early Childhood Development*, National Research Council and Institute of Medicine, Washington, D.C.: The National Academy Press, 2000. Online at www.nap.edu/books/0309069882/html/ (as of February 2004).

Provides an overview of new research on the effects on child development of nature versus nurture, the home environment, and the costs and benefits of early childhood intervention. Reviews the evidence of "brain wiring" and how children learn to speak, think, and regulate their behavior.

Differences in Children's Math and Reading Skills Across Service Planning Areas

Los Angeles County is divided into eight service planning areas (SPAs), which are geographical regions within the county. For more information on SPAs and a map, see www.childpc.org. The residents of SPAs within Los Angeles County differ considerably by income, educational attainment, ethnicity, and many other characteristics. SPAs also differ in the types of libraries, children's literacy programs, preschools, and other facilities and programs available to parents and children.

Table C.1 shows how children in each SPA are doing on school-readiness measures and on early literacy environment and parenting behavior variables. We also show information on the socioeconomic characteristics of each SPA.

Table C.1
Social and School-Readiness-Related Variables by SPA

Variables	Antelope SPA 1	San Fernando SPA 2	San Gabriel SPA 3	Metro SPA 4	West SPA 5	South SPA 6	East SPA 7	South Bay SPA 8
Social characteristics								
% in poverty	16	14	14	26	12	32	16	17
% foreign born	15	37	38	51	28	35	38	29
% adults with college education	22	35	33	28	58	12	19	34
% white	51	48	27	22	63	3	19	33
% Latino	29	36	45	54	16	60	68	35
% African American	13	4	5	6	6	35	3	16
% Asian/Pacific Islander	3	9	23	15	11	2	8	13
% Native American	1	0.3	0.3	0.3	0.2	0.2	0.3	0.3
% other	3	4	2	2	4	1	2	3
School-readiness measures								
Reading scores (%)								
High	0	26	7	10	49	10	21	24
Middle	47	60	60	64	49	64	63	56
Low	53	14	33	26	2	26	16	20
Math scores (%)								
High	14	42	14	13	66	14	15	23
Middle	59	38	42	55	32	52	51	47
Low	27	20	54	32	2	34	34	30
% with sad/anxious behavior	20	18	31	30	6	47	21	25
% with aggressive behavior	37	16	18	18	6	32	25	22
Home environment and parenting								
Mother reads to child 3+ times per week (%)								
Toddlers	71	61	56	61	88	26	39	57
Preschoolers	53	53	55	58	75	44	82	64
Someone else reads to child 3+ times per week (%)								
Toddlers	31	39	49	29	70	34	31	51
Preschoolers	40	31	49	30	68	34	41	40
Child has minimum number of books (%)								
Toddlers	100	89	92	85	100	59	77	89
Preschoolers	88	75	77	65	100	56	78	72
Average hours of TV watched per day								
Toddlers	1.70	2.50	2.40	2.19	1.54	2.15	2.18	2.38
Preschoolers	3.31	2.39	2.14	3.27	0.86	3.26	2.52	2.35
Child visits library several times per year (%)								
Preschoolers	32	54	58	43	77	37	64	52
Parenting behavior (%)								
Praises child almost every day	75	71	63	73	91	42	60	64
Hugs child almost every day	85	88	86	96	96	86	88	92
Says something positive about child to someone else almost every day	46	59	48	63	70	39	49	52
Spanked child at least once in past week	31	23	26	22	8	33	29	22
Sent child to room at least once in past week	53	53	46	27	15	42	40	34

SOURCE: Social variables are from the Los Angeles Children's Planning Council web site at www.childpc.org. Other data come from L.A.FANS tabulations for each SPA.

Description of School-Readiness Measures from L.A.FANS

L.A.FANS included a number of measures related to school readiness. Results reported in this book are based on the following three measures:

- Home Observation for Measurement of the Environment, an assessment of a child's home environment
- Behavior Problem Index, a measure of social and emotional development
- Woodcock-Johnson-Revised Test of Achievement, a measure of language reading and math skills.

Home Observation for Measurement of the Environment

The Home Observation for Measurement of the Environment (HOME) is a widely used and reliable tool to assess those aspects of the emotional and learning environment in a child's home that contribute to school readiness.[43] It consists of parental responses to questions and the interviewer's observations of the home environment. For this book, we used responses from the HOME to measure both the child's home literacy environment and parenting practices.

For the child's home literacy environment, we asked parents, usually mothers, to answer questions that told us about the number of books a child owns, how often the mother or another relative reads to the child, and how much television the child watches. We also asked each mother of a preschooler how often the child visits the library and whether the mother discusses TV programs with the child. Table D.1 shows the HOME questions on the home literacy environment that we used for L.A.FANS.

To measure parenting behavior, we used other questions included in the HOME. These questions are shown in Table D.2.

For the statistical analysis in Chapter Five, answers to these five parenting behavior questions were combined into a warmth index and a discipline index for each respondent, using a statistical method called principal components analysis. This type of analysis provides a method for combining items into indexes based on the intercorrelation among the items. Note that we have used abbreviated versions of the standard HOME warmth and discipline scale (which include a number of additional items) to make the results easier to understand.

Table D.1
HOME Questions on the Home Literacy Environment in L.A.FANS

Questions	Asked for toddlers	Asked for preschoolers
How often do you get a chance to read to your child?	✓	✓
How often do other family members get a chance to read to your child?	✓	✓
About how many children's books does your child have?	✓	✓
About how often does your child go to the library?		✓
How much time would you say your child spends watching television or videos on a typical weekday, either in your home or somewhere else?	✓	✓
When your family watches TV together, how often do you discuss TV programs with your child?		✓

Table D.2
HOME Questions on Parenting Behavior in L.A.FANS

Questions	Warmth scale	Discipline scale
In the past week, about how many times have you praised your child for doing something worthwhile?	✓	
In the past week, have you shown your child physical affection (for example: kisses, hugs, stroking hair, etc.)?	✓	
In the past week, how many times have you told another adult (for example: spouse, friend, coworker, visitor, relative) something positive about your child?	✓	
In the past week, how many times have you had to spank your child?		✓
In the past week, how many times have you put/sent your child in/to her room or another room as a punishment?		✓

Behavior Problem Index

The BPI[44] is a well-tested measure of a child's emotional and behavioral development. It was adapted by the Achenbach Child Behavior Checklist[45] for use in large-scale child development surveys. It was designed to assess children's problems such as anxiety, depression, and aggression that are associated with their readiness for school.

For the BPI measure used for L.A.FANS, a parent—typically the mother—was presented with a list of 28 statements and then asked how true each one was for her child. The statements measure the following two primary types of behavior problems:

- *Inwardly expressed* (internalizing) behaviors, such as sadness and feelings of inadequacy. For example, a parent is given the statement—"My child felt or complained that no one loved her"—and is asked to rate the statement as: often true, sometimes true, not true at all. Previous studies have linked a child's depressive (internalizing) behavior with poor school performance.[46] Other studies show that depressed and anxious children tend to be less engaged in the classroom and to have fewer friends, all of which have negative consequences for a child's school performance.
- *Outwardly expressed* (externalizing) behaviors, such as aggressiveness and a tendency to lie, cheat, or express hostility. Here the parent is given a statement such as—"My child bullied or has been cruel or mean to others"—and is asked to rate the statement as: often true, sometimes true, not true at all. Children with higher levels of aggressive behavior may experience more problems in school because they act out, pay less attention, and may not get along with teachers and other pupils.

The parents' ratings of the statements are summed for each type of problem, and this produces a BPI score that reflects the frequency of the problems. These scores are then turned into percentile scores, for example, a score of 85 percent indicates that the child has more problems than 85 percent of the children assessed.

Woodcock-Johnson-Revised Test of Achievement

L.A.FANS used the Woodcock-Johnson-Revised Test of Achievement (WJ-R ACH),[47] a standardized and widely used battery of tests to assess children's language development and math skills. Studies show that this measure is a reliable test of a child's reading and problem-solving ability. Children were given the following two tests:

- *Letter-Word Identification:* This test consists of two parts—picture-matching and identification of novel words. For instance, children were shown a picture and were asked to match the picture to a word shown on a list. Also, children of appropriate age were asked to read a list of words. The level of difficulty increases as the child progresses through the test.
- *Applied Problems:* This test assesses the child's mathematical reasoning skills. The child is presented with a description of a problem to be solved. To do this test, the child must be able to perform simply counting, addition, and subtraction.

Both tests were administered to children ages three through five and calibrated to each child's age and ability. Tests were administered in English and Spanish, depending on the language in which the child felt more comfortable.

To assess parental literacy levels, L.A.FANS also administered the passage comprehension test from the WJ-R ACH. This test was given to the child's primary caretaker (usually the mother). It consists of two parts: picture identification and passage completion. First, the test taker is asked to identify a picture that represents a phrase read aloud by the examiner. Next, the test taker is required to read a short, incomplete passage and then provide a key word that would complete the passage.

The scores from the WJ-R ACH are "norm referenced" rather than "standards referenced." This means that children in the L.A.FANS sample are compared with children their own age in a nationally representative sample, instead of being assessed relative to a minimum level of reading and math skills that is required to be "ready for school." Norm-referenced standards provide an assessment of whether a child's reading or problem-solving skills are "age appropriate." The children analyzed in the WJ-R-based part of this book are three to five years old. Relatively few three-year-olds are likely to meet a fixed minimum skills level for school readiness because they are so young. Similarly, four-year-olds are less likely than five-year-olds to have reached a fixed minimum skills level for school readiness. Norm-referenced standards allow us to assess children ages three and five using the same criterion—whether or not the child's skills are below, at, or above the national average for her age. However, norm-referenced standards do not allow us to identify children who are or are not ready for school, based on a minimum skills level, on the day they are tested.

The Woodcock-Johnson procedures classify children according to the schema in Table D.3.

We have collapsed this schema into three categories for this book: High (including the first three categories), middle (the "average" or "normal" category), and low (including the bottom three categories). Children are considered to be performing at an age-appropriate level if they are in the middle category.[48]

Table D.3 Woodcock-Johnson Classification Table			
Standard Score	Percentile rank	WJ-R classification	Alternate labels
131–135	98 to 99.9	Very superior	Very high
121–130	92 to 97	Superior	Well above average
111–120	76 to 91	High average	Above average
90–110	25 to 75	Average	Normal
80–89	9 to 24	Low average	Below average
70–79	3 to 8	Low	Poor
69 and below	1 to 2	Very low	Deficient

SOURCE: R. W. Woodcock and N. Mather, "WJ-R Test of Achievement: Examiner's Manual," in R. W. Woodcock and M. B. Johnson, *Woodcock-Johnson Psycho-Educational Battery-Revised*, Itasca, Ill.: Riverside, 1989 (rev. 1990).

Endnotes

[1] The NEGP is a federal agency established by Congress that is in charge of setting national education goals and monitoring progress toward these goals. For more information, go to www.negp.gov.

[2] For reviews of the importance of school readiness to success in school and in life, see National Education Goals Panel, *Getting a Good Start in School*, Washington, D.C.: National Education Goals Panel, 1997; M. Susan Burns, Peg Griffin, and Catherine E. Snow, eds., *Starting Out Right: A Guide to Promoting Children's Reading Success*, Committee on the Prevention of Reading Difficulties in Young Children, Commission on Behavioral and Social Sciences and Education, National Research Council, Washington, D.C.: The National Academy Press, 1999; and Barbara T. Bowman, M. Suzanne Donovan, and M. Susan Burns, eds., *Eager to Learn: Educating Our Preschoolers*, Commission on Behavioral and Social Sciences and Education, National Research Council, Washington, D.C.: The National Academy Press, 2001.

[3] For more information on the link between school performance and involvement in crime and antisocial behavior, see A. McEvoy and R. Welker, "Antisocial Behavior, Academic Failure, and School Climate: A Critical Review," *Journal of Emotional & Behavioral Disorders*, Vol. 8, No. 3, 2000, pp. 130–140; C. M. Schaeffer, H. Petras, N. Ialongo, J. Poduska, and S. Kellam, "Modeling Growth in Boys' Aggressive Behavior Across Elementary School: Links to Later Criminal Involvement, Conduct Disorder, and Antisocial Personality Disorder," *Developmental Psychology*, Vol. 39, No. 6, 2003, pp. 1020–1035; and A. J. Reynolds, J. A. Temple, D. L. Robertson, and E. A. Mann, "Long-Term Effects of an Early Childhood Intervention on Educational Achievement and Juvenile Arrest," *Journal of the American Medical Association*, Vol. 285, No. 18, 2001, pp. 2339–2346.

[4] National Education Goals Panel, 1997; Burns, Griffin, and Snow, 1999; and Bowman, Donovan, and Burns, 2001.

[5] For more information, see Lynn A. Karoly et al., *Investing in Our Children: What We Know and Don't Know About the Costs and Benefits of Early Childhood Interventions*, Santa Monica, Calif.: RAND Corporation, 1998. Online at www.rand.org/publications/MR/MR898/ (as of February 2004); and Lynn A. Karoly et al., *Assessing Costs and Benefits of Early Childhood Intervention Programs: Overview and Application to the Starting Early Starting Smart Program*, Santa Monica, Calif.: RAND Corporation, 2001. Online at www.rand.org/publications/MR/MR1336/ (as of February 2004).

[6] C. Wood, "Parent-Child Preschool Activities Can Affect the Development of Literacy Skills," *Journal of Research in Reading*, Vol. 25, No. 3, 2002, pp. 241–258; V. J. Molfese, A. Modglin, and D. L. Molfese, "The Role of Environment in the Development of Reading Skills: A Longitudinal Study of Preschool and School-Age Measures," *Journal of Learning Disabilities*, Vol. 36, No. 1, 2003, pp. 59–67; M. A. Gartstein and B. I. Fagot, "Parental Depression, Parenting and Family Adjustment, and Child Effortful Control: Explaining Externalizing Behaviors for Preschool Children," *Journal of Applied Developmental Psychology*, Vol. 24, No. 2, 2003, pp. 143–177; and B. P. Ackerman, E. Brown, and C. E. Izard, "Continuity and Change in Levels of Externalizing Behavior in School Children from Economically Disadvantaged Families," *Child Development*, Vol. 74, No. 3, 2003, pp. 694–709.

[7] Karoly et al., 1998; C. E. Cunningham, R. Bremner, and M. Boyle, "Large Group Community-Based Parenting Programs for Families of Preschoolers at Risk for Disruptive Disorders: Utilization, Cost Effectiveness, and Outcome," *Journal of Child Psychology and Psychiatry*, Vol. 36, 1995, pp. 1141–1159; and N. Baydar, M. J. Reid, and C. Webster-Stratton, "The Role of Mental Health Factors and Program Engagement in the Effectiveness of a Preventive Parenting Program for Head Start Mothers," *Child Development*, Vol. 74, No. 5, 2003, pp. 1433–1453.

[8] Molfese, Modglin, and Molfese, 2003; Wood, 2002; and M. A. Evans, D. Shaw, and M. Bell, "Home Literacy Activities and Their Influence on Early Literacy Skills," *Canadian Journal of Experimental Psychology*, Vol. 54, 2000, pp. 65–75.

[9] R. H. Bradley and R. F. Corwyn, *HOME Inventory*, Little Rock, Ark.: University of Arkansas, not dated. See www.ualr.edu/~crtldept/home4.htm.

[10] M. Senechal, J. LeFevre, E. Thomas, and K. Daley, "Differential Effects of Home Literacy Experiences on the Development of Oral and Written Language," *Reading Research Quarterly*, Vol. 32, 1998, pp. 96–116.

[11] See Molfese, Modglin, and Molfese, 2003.

[12] A. T. Clark and B. E. Kurtz-Costes, "Television Viewing, Educational Quality of the Home Environment, and School Readiness," *Journal of Educational Research*, Vol. 90, 1997, pp. 279–285; J. C. Wright, A. C. Huston, K. C. Murphy, M. St. Peters, M. Pinon, R. Scantlin, and J. Kotler, "The Relations of Early Television Viewing to School Readiness and Vocabulary of Children from Low-Income Families: The Early Window Project," *Child Development*, Vol. 72, No. 5, 2001, pp. 1347–1356. The American Academy of Pediatrics recommends no TV for children age 2 and younger. For older preschoolers, the academy recommends "no more than 1 to 2 hours per day of educational, nonviolent programs" (see www.aap.org/family/tv1.htm, last accessed February 2004).

[13] Molfese, Modglin, and Molfese, 2003; R. H. Bradley, R. F. Corwyn, M. Burchinal, H. Pipes McAdoo, and C. Garcia Coll, "The Home Environments of Children in the United States Part II: Relations with Behavioral Development Through Age Thirteen," *Child Development*, Vol. 72, 2001, pp. 1868–1886; B. M. Caldwell and R. H. Bradley, "The Relation of Infants' Home Environments to Achievement Test Performance in First Grade: A Follow-Up Study," *Child Development*, Vol. 55, No. 3, 1984b, pp. 803–809.

[14] Of the mothers in the L.A.FANS sample, 35 percent did not finish high school.

[15] J. Brooks-Gunn, G. J. Duncan, and J. L. Aber, eds., *Neighborhood Poverty: Vol. 1, Context and Consequences for Children*, New York, N.Y.: Russell Sage Foundation, 1997; R. J. Sampson, J. D. Morenoff, and T. Gannon-Rowley, "Assessing 'Neighborhood Effects': Social Processes and New Directions in Research," *Annual Review of Sociology*, Vol. 28, 2002, pp. 1–51.

[16] National Education Goals Panel, 1997; and Burns, Griffin, and Snow, 1999.

[17] R. W. Woodcock and N. Mather, "WJ-R Test of Achievement: Examiner's Manual," in R. W. Woodcock and M. B. Johnson, *Woodcock-Johnson Psycho-Educational Battery-Revised*, Itasca, Ill.: Riverside, 1989 (rev. 1990).

[18] See Appendix D for more information.

[19] Figures 3.5 and 3.6 show predicted test scores for different categories of maternal education and home literacy activities while holding other independent variables constant at their means.

[20] Ackerman, Brown, and Izard, 2003; Bradley et al., 2001; E. Maccoby and J. Martin, "Socialization in the Context of the Family: Parent-Child Interactions," in E. M. Hetherington, ed., *Handbook of Child Psychology: Vol. 4, Socialization, Personality, and Social Development*, New York, N.Y.: Wiley, 1983, pp. 1–101.

[21] Maccoby and Martin, 1983.

[22] These measures are based on questions from the HOME inventory, which is described in Sandraluz Lara-Cinisomo and Anne R. Pebley, *Los Angeles County Young Children's Literacy Experiences, Emotional Well-Being and Skills Acquisition: Results from the Los Angeles Family and Neighborhood Survey*, Santa Monica, Calif.: RAND Corporation, DRU-3041-LAFANS, 2003. Online at www.rand.org/labor/DRU/DRU3041.pdf.

[23] Bradley et al., 2001.

[24] Maccoby and Martin, 1983.

[25] Bradley et al., 2001.

[26] X. Chen, K. H. Rubin, and B. Li, "Depressed Mood in Chinese Children: Relations with School Performance and Family Environment," *Journal of Consulting and Clinical Psychology*, Vol. 63, 1995, pp. 938–947; K. Coolahan, J. Fantuzzo, J. Mendez, and P. McDermott, "Preschool Peer Interactions and Readiness to Learn: Relationships Between Classroom Peer Play and Learning Behaviors and Conduct," *Journal of Educational Psychology*, Vol. 92, No. 3, 2000, pp. 458–465; J. J. Wood, P. A. Cowan, and B. L. Baker, "Behavior Problems and Peer Rejection in Preschool Boys and Girls," *The Journal of Genetic Psychology*, Vol. 163, No. 1, 2002, pp. 72–88; M. Willoughby, J. Kupersmidt, and D. Bryant, "Overt and Covert Dimensions of Antisocial Behavior in Early Childhood," *Journal of Abnormal Child Psychology*, Vol. 29, No. 3, 2001, pp. 177–187.

[27] See: Jack P. Shonkoff and Deborah A. Phillips, eds., *From Neurons to Neighborhoods: The Science of Early Childhood Development*, National Research Council and Institute of Medicine, Washington, D.C.: The National Academy Press, 2000. Online at www.nap.edu/books/0309069882/html/ (as of February 2004).

[28] Bowman, Donovan, and Burns, 2001.

[29] Each parent can reply (1) often true, (2) sometimes true, (3) not true. Children get a one if the parent says sometimes true, a two if often true, and a zero otherwise. Then all the items are added. There are 11 items in the sadness/anxiety scale, so the scores go from 0 to 22. There were 15 items in the aggressive behavior scale, so the scores go from 0 to 30.

[30] Center for Human Resource Research, Ohio State University, NLYS79 (*National Longitudinal Survey of Youth 1979) Child & Young Adult Data User Guide*, Columbus, Ohio: Center for Human Resource Research, Ohio State University, 1998 (rev. 2000).

[31] A complete breakdown of these scales is available in Lara-Cinisomo and Pebley, 2003.

[32] R. H. Bradley and R. F. Corwyn, "Socioeconomic Status and Child Development," *Annual Review of Psychology*, Vol. 53, 2002, pp. 371–399.

[33] Indexes for discipline and for warmth were created using separate principal components analyses (one for the discipline variables and the other for the warmth variables). Principal components analysis is a type of statistical analysis that uses the patterns of correlation among variables to create an index. The multivariate analysis includes the first principal component for each aspect of parenting as continuous variables.

[34] Figures 5.1, 5.2, 5.3, 5.4, and 5.5 show predicted behavior problems scale scores for different categories of neighborhood poverty and parenting behavior while holding other independent variables constant at their means.

[35] Note: The discipline index included in this analysis is a continuous variable (from the principal components analysis). To illustrate the effects of different levels on the discipline index, we calculated the predicted behavior problems index for each type of child behavior at three points along the discipline index: the mean, one standard deviation below the mean, and one standard deviation above the mean of the discipline index.

[36] Note: The warmth index included in this analysis is a continuous variable (from the principal components analysis). To illustrate the effects of different levels on the warmth index, we calculated the predicted behavior problems index for each type of child behavior at three points along the warmth index: the mean, one standard deviation below the mean, and one standard deviation above the mean of the warmth index.

[37] See note 35 above.

[38] Bradley et al., 2001; Cunningham, Bremner, and Boyle, 1995; Baydar, Reid, and Webster-Stratton, 2003.

[39] Anne R. Pebley and Narayan Sastry, *Concentrated Poverty vs. Concentrated Affluence: Effects on Neighborhood Social Environments and Children's Outcomes*, Santa Monica, Calif.: RAND Corporation, DRU-2400/10-LAFANS, 2003. Online at www.rand.org/labor/DRU/DRU2400.10.pdf.

[40] J. Brooks-Gunn, L. Berlin, and A. Fuligni, "Early Childhood Intervention Programs: What About the Family?" in J. P. Shonkoff and S. J. Meisels, eds., *Handbook of Early Childhood Intervention*, 2nd edition, New York, N.Y.: Cambridge University Press, 2000.

[41] D. Gomby, P. Culross, and R. Behrman, "Home Visiting: Recent Program Evaluations—Analysis and Recommendations," *The Future of Children*, Vol. 9, No. 1, 1999, pp. 4–26.

[42] Janet Currie, *Early Childhood Intervention Programs: What Do We Know?* Los Angeles, Calif.: UCLA and NBER, 2000. Online at www.jcpr.org/wp/wpprofile.cfm?id=176. See also Karoly et al., 1998.

[43] B. M. Caldwell and R. H. Bradley, *Home Observation for Measurement of the Environment*, Little Rock, Ark.: University of Arkansas, 1984a.

[44] James L. Peterson and Nicholas Zill, "Marital Disruption, Parent-Child Relationships, and Behavior Problems in Children," *Journal of Marriage and the Family*, Vol. 48, 1986, pp. 295–307.

[45] T. Achenbach and C. Edelbrock, "Behavioral Problems and Competencies Reported by Parents of Normal and Disturbed Children Aged Four Through Sixteen," *Monographs of the Society for Research in Child Development*, Vol. 46, Issue 1, No. 188, 1981.

[46] N. S. Ialongo, G. Edelsohn, and S. G. Kellan, "A Further Look at the Prognostic Power of Young Children's Reports of Depressed Mood and Feelings," *Child Development*, Vol. 72, No. 3, 2001, pp. 736–747.

[47] Woodcock and Johnson, 1989.

[48] Woodcock and Johnson, 1989.